REAL MOMENTS

BOB DYLAN
BY BARRY FEINSTEIN

Acknowledgements

My thanks and enormous gratitude go to my friend
and agent Dave Brolan without whose help and support
I never would have completed this project.

A very special thank you to Pete Mauney
for his talent in bringing these photographs to life
from the original negatives.

There will never be enough gratitude for the friendship and
support from friends and family throughout the years: Charles
& Aviva Blaichman, Jack & Catherine Glazer, Lola Cohen &
Mathew Rudicoff, Tom & Vivian Kay, Mickey & Lynn Saewitz,
Peter & Kerry Bogart, Tommy & Gill Lipuma, Stewart & Ruth
Levine, Tina Bromberg, Donnie Brice, Tad Wise, Roger Vaughan,
Al Q., Larry & Christy Sloman, Vincent Donelon & Chris
McCabe, Mitchell (Pep) Weiss, Bella Sekons, Claudia Levy, Bruce
Cohen, Jeff & Colleen Cohen, Susan Schweitzman, Tina
Firestone, David & Nikki Goldbeck, Marsha Fleisher & Bananas,
Bob Neuwirth, Cydne Cort, Ester Lisker, Joel Gilbert, Holly Coe,
Michelle Esrick & Emory Joseph, Robin Harvey & George
Acober, Thomas Donavon, Buddy Anderson, Jim Dickson,
Richard Serafian, Larry & Paula Poons, Jim Marshall, Kate
Simon, Richard & Marcia Leeds, Jim Starlin and Sonny Lan

And to all my children: Alicia, Erika & Alex, Jake,
Jasper & Chelsea; and my grandchildren: Jules, Emmett
and brand new baby Nick.

Signed fine art prints of many of these images are available from
www.barryfeinsteinphotography.com

This book is dedicated to my extraordinary mother Rose, who
just left us at the age of 99 and remained an admirer of Dylan's
work till the end – and to my loving and immensely talented
wife Judith, who has been there every step of the way.

REAL
MOMENTS

BOB DYLAN
BY BARRY FEINSTEIN

VISION ON

BERLIN | COPENHAGEN | LONDON | LOS ANGELES | MADRID | NEW YORK | PARIS | SYDNEY | TOKYO

Foreword

Dylan with Bob Neuwirth, 1966

Some people see things – others can't. Barry Feinstein has an eye. Exactly where or when he developed his vision is irrelevant. We are the lucky ones as a result.

Perhaps bouncing around the Southern Californian desert back trails with motorcycle pals, Dave and Bud Ekins and Steve McQueen helped. Or slipping behind the "iron curtain" for the first images of Cold War Poland (as yet regrettably unpublished, by the way), or covering Hollywood with an uncompromising lens during the civil rights protests of the early '60s. Maybe it was while shooting the many classic album covers for which he is so well known. In any case Barry has an instinct for the unique capture.

Many can point a camera and push a button. Not everyone can make an image sing. Like a great song, a great photograph should have something to say. Sometimes it's a sense of being really there, a record of a moment in time or sometimes a conveyance of the voice of the artist that verges on poetry.

I first met Barry Feinstein at his photography studio on 73rd St. in Manhattan in what was then still New York City. There was an immaculate, bright red, 101 Indian Scout, vintage 1929 motorcycle in the corner. This was the first time I had seen a bike displayed as a dedicated work of art.

In Woodstock, New York, late at night he let me ride his 1968 Triumph Bonneville 650 TT Special that had been modified at the Ekins' shop into a bored-out 750cc rocket. When I let out the clutch the beast nearly left me sitting in mid-air. After a short, loud (and very quick) ride through the surrounding hills I got it home in one piece and was ranting about its torque and speed capabilities in Albert and Sally's kitchen when suddenly the driveway filled with flashing red and blue lights. Town constable, county sheriffs (two counties) and New York state troopers all wanted to know who owned the bike that had people awake in the middle of the quiet mountain night. Barry owned up and with a stream of biker technical info he charmed the law down and out of giving me a nasty set of moving violations. His bikes always seemed a mix of classic and custom – like his life and his images.

The book you have in your hands contains a series of photos taken at different times, the majority during a 1966 tour during which Bob was accompanied by members of The Band (minus Levon Helm who was substituted for by Mickey Jones). This was Bob's first electric tour of Europe after the 1965 acoustic tour documented by D.A. Pennebaker's *Don't Look Back*. Barry's accompanying captions explain the circumstances, his camera tells the story.

As you look at these images I hope you can see what Barry Feinstein sees.

Bob Neuwirth, New York
January, 2008

Introduction

Dylan, Liverpool, 1966

I don't feel that much needs explaining as my photographs speak for themselves.

Bob and I were friends long before we worked together. We hung out and understood each other. When there was something to say we would talk, when there wasn't we were silent. We were similar in that way, no bullshit.

That's the way it is in music. What often makes a piece of music great are the notes left out. And it's like that with photography; knowing when to take a shot and, more importantly, when not to. I wanted my pictures to say something. I don't really like stand-up portraits, there's nothing there, no life, no feeling. I was much more interested in capturing real moments.

I was in a unique position, given complete access and trust during a very special period. I saw Bob perform hundreds of times, travelled with him, often spent 24 hours a day with him. Sometimes there were thousands of people at a concert, others times it was just the two of us.

The mutual trust, respect and friendship we had for each other are reflected in these photographs. I liked his work, he liked mine. He knew I would make him look interesting – and he was interesting. I knew I was in the presence of genius.

Barry Feinstein
Woodstock, New York
January, 2008

"I knew immediately it was a very unusual shot and an angle, and a moment with Bob"

New York City, 1963
(right)

Columbia asked me to do an album cover, so I took Bob up to my friend John Cort's penthouse apartment in New York City. I said, 'Let's go to the edge on the balcony and make some pictures.' I was kneeling down and I said to Bob, 'Look around, look at the landscape, the city and this and that. I went click, click, click. I didn't have to shoot a lot of pictures because I knew immediately it was a very unusual shot and an angle, and a moment with Bob. We looked at the proof sheet and he chose that shot. In those days the record company normally chose the picture for the cover, especially Columbia, but they let him do it this time. They did a good job. It wasn't premeditated or anything, it was one of the quickest and easiest photo sessions I've ever done.

"I was taking pictures for myself, not for a magazine or anything"

New York City, 1964
(left)

With Mimi Farina, 1964
(above)

I met Joan Baez through Bob backstage before one of her concerts with Mimi Farina, Joan's sister. Bob was playing the autoharp, Mimi just listening. I was taking pictures for myself, not for a magazine or anything.

Ireland, 1966

We were in Ireland, travelling
between Dublin and Belfast,
the only time I've ever been on
a train in one country where
you had to go through customs.
I couldn't understand it, it was
pretty weird, they didn't give
us any trouble though, just let
us through. There were only a
few shows, Belfast and Dublin,
but he was very popular, they
loved him there and really
appreciated the acoustic music.
We got out a bit and looked
at the countryside.

"Backstage before shows, I don't recall him getting nervous, it was quite relaxed"

Birmingham, 1966

Backstage before shows, I don't recall him really getting nervous or anything, it was quite relaxed. We tried to keep as many people away as possible… there were always a lot of press and fans, managers, musicians, everybody. We didn't travel with a big crew; it was the band, Dylan, the sound guy, maybe about 15-20 people, but we had a whole film crew. Every time you scratched your head someone took a picture of you. I think it helped the film crew having me there, made them more comfortable. At times Bob didn't want to be filmed, but I never ran into that myself. Bob was good, he would go along with anything you needed. I think that's what made the pictures I did different, because he knew I wouldn't use anything unless it was to his advantage.

"Hair was the important thing in those days"

London, 1966

(previous page and right)

We went out shopping in Carnaby Street looking for some new clothes. He was quite taken with the place. The staff were very pleasant. Bob knew exactly what he wanted; as soon as he saw it he bought it.

Paris, 1966

(previous page)

Backstage at L'Olympia. That's Bob's manager Albert Grossman, French rock'n'roller Johnny Hallyday and singer Françoise Hardy (with her back to the camera) and the English tour manager. They got on great. They all liked each other.

London, 1966

(right)

This was taken in a boot shop on Carnaby Street. Bob did buy a few pairs of boots. There were some publicity photos of big name artists on the wall and his was on there by the time we left!

L'Olympia, Paris, 1966

This happened all the time;
people loved to look at him.
They thought maybe something
was going to come out of his
mouth and be different. If they
asked him something sensible,
he gave them a decent answer.
If they asked a bullshit question
he gave them a bullshit answer.
It just came with the territory
as far as he was concerned.
He went along with it… except
if it was totally bullshitty and
he would tell them.

"Bob was very perceptive. What he cared about was getting the right moment"

Birmingham, 1966

(previous page)

This looks like *The Last Supper*, back at the hotel somewhere in England, with the band and crew. Bob didn't care about publicity pictures if he knew you and trusted you. He knew my philosophy and knew I wouldn't make him look like an asshole. He was very perceptive. What he cared about was getting the right moment.

Cardiff, Wales, 1966

(left and below)

I like the shape, the design of this shot [below]. The old theory is that if you throw enough bullshit at a wall some of it will stick, but I didn't do that. I waited.

Birmingham, 1966

(previous page)

This was the worst meal I ever had, the most disgusting food – fish soup. I said, 'Hold it before you throw up'.

Scotland, 1966

(right)

The kitchen staff didn't have a clue who Bob was, but they were happy to have their photo taken with him.

England, 1966

(previous page)

When Bob was performing, I'd watch from the side of the stage. I didn't take many live shots. I was just there to make good pictures. I shot all the shows, but I picked the moment carefully. The shows were thrilling. Some nights were better than others. On some he was happier and if you were on the tour you'd notice.

Paris, 1966

(right)

Bob with Albert Grossman. I got to meet Bob through Mary Travers who was managed by Albert Grossman. I shot some of his other artists too: Peter, Paul & Mary, Gordon Lightfoot, Odetta. Albert had good taste; he knew who was going to make it. It was interesting to watch him. He was some piece of work; very loyal.

L'Olympia, Paris, 1966

In Paris, backstage at
L'Olympia, a fan caught Bob
at one of his easy moments
and he took this big poster and
autographed it for them. He was
happy to do it. He was alright
with the fans

Royal Albert Hall, London, 1966

(right and below)

I didn't really enjoy taking performance pictures, they weren't my cup of tea. If you want to see a performance, buy a ticket. Bob looks good here though. It's one of the nicer live shots that I have.

Savoy Hotel, London, 1966

This is the Savoy Hotel in London. Bob picked up Pennebaker's movie camera. He loved shooting with it, but I don't know if any of his footage made the cut.

Newcastle City Hall, 1966

(left)

I never used a flash in my photography. I shot using black and white film; colour can be deceptive. This tour lent itself to black and white – it was journalistic, reportage, verité! Even when the shot is dark and shadowy, it's more real. This was Bob playing the piano and really getting lost in the music.

Ireland, 1966

(right)

Bob was being interviewed. This is a very passive, beautiful picture of him.

Sheffield, 1966
(this page and overleaf)

We saw this big store front with the letters 'LSD'. We stopped to check it out. It was a betting shop. Bob went inside to see what it was like but he didn't place a bet. 'LSD' was very symbolic.

"'LSD' was very symbolic"

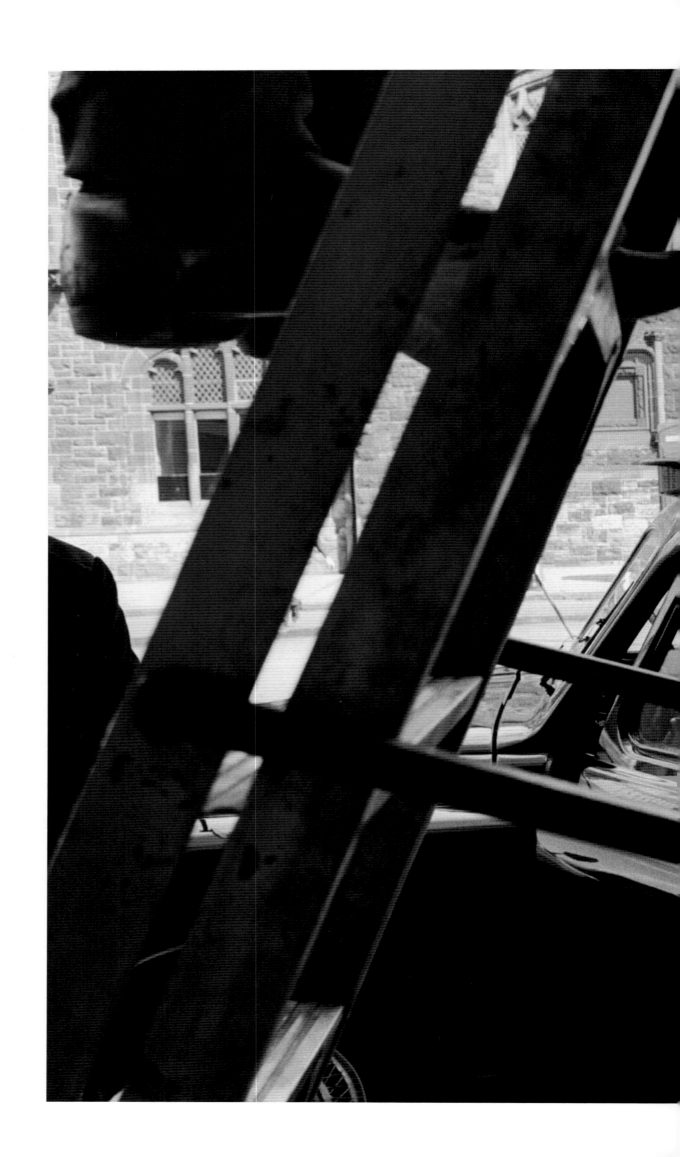

England, 1966

"He loved those kids. He was compassionate to them, they were like waifs."

Liverpool, 1966
(this page and overleaf)

Bob felt great in Liverpool. The scenery, the houses, the open spaces were wonderful. He got all athletic throwing these rocks around. I said, 'It's Bowling For Dollars!' He loved those kids. He was compassionate to them. They were like waifs. It was the day of the FA Cup Final, 14 May (Everton v Sheffield Wednesday). I asked if he wanted a photo with them and he said sure, so we found a doorway of this old warehouse. The kids were just playing in the street; they just got in there wherever they could stand. They posed themselves and it became a famous picture. The BBC tracked all the kids down recently and recreated the shot. None of them knew who Bob was. It reminds me of the Art Kane *Great Day In Harlem* shot with all the jazz guys.

Liverpool, 1966
(left and below)

"Bob felt great in Liverpool. The scenery, the houses, the open spaces were wonderful"

Liverpool, 1966
(this page and overleaf)

I said to Bob, 'You look
through my camera and
I'll stand in the doorway
and you'll see what
you're going to look like'
[overleaf]. He could see
what I was seeing. He
loved it. Looking up, the
perspective was incredible.
Sometimes I would do that.
When I thought it was going
to look great; I would have
him look through the camera
to take at look at what he
was going to look like. This
area of Liverpool was great –
it had space, dimension,
old buildings, vacant lots...
everything for great shots.

"Bob got all athletic throwing these rocks around. I said, 'It's Bowling For Dollars!'"

Scotland, 1966
(previous page)

**Royal Albert
Hall, 1966**
(right)

"He was a believer in going forward, not doing the same show every time"

England, 1966
(above and right)

He made the change to electric and just did his thing. He was upset that some people didn't get it. In Scotland a girl fan even punched him, but he was a believer in doing something and going forward, not doing the same show every time. Do that, you get nowhere. By the end of the show everyone loved it though.

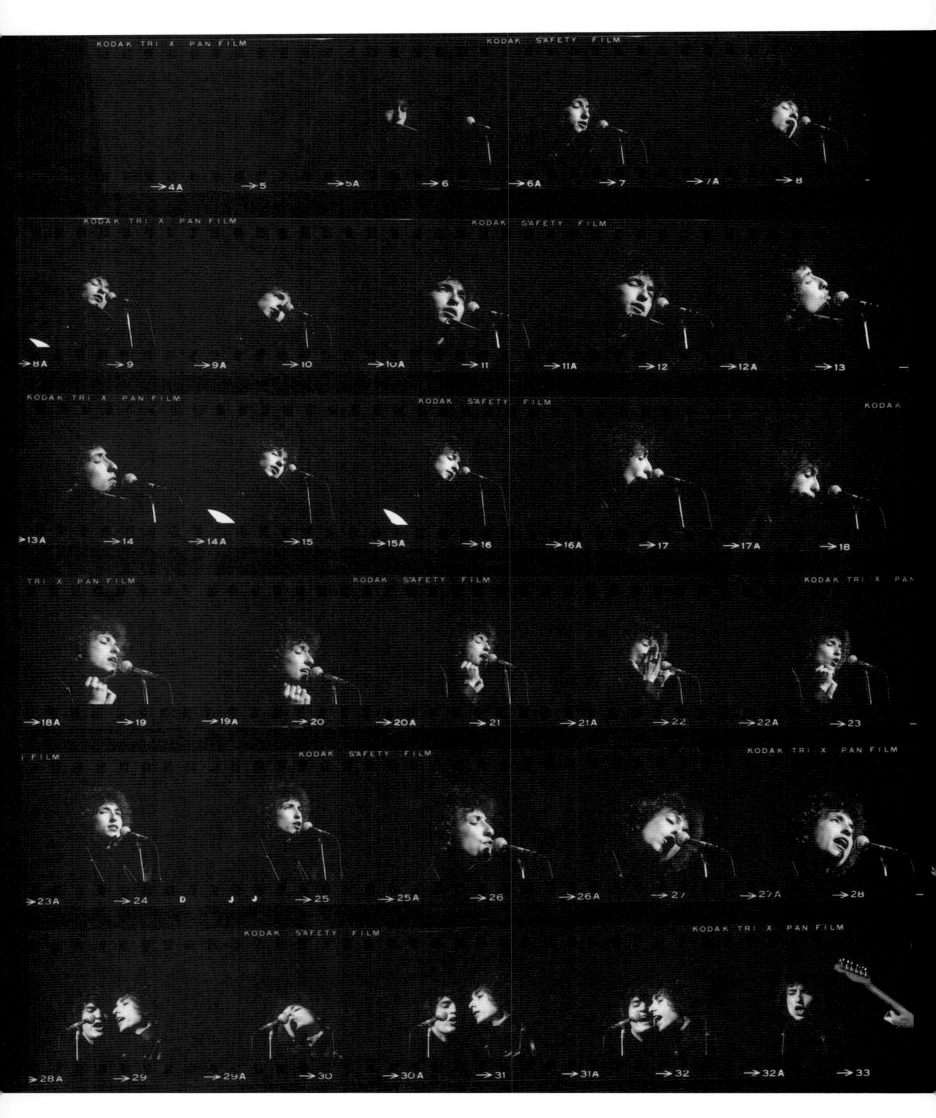

Newcastle, 1966

(left and below)

Contact sheet from City Hall shows Bob singing 'One Too Many Mornings' with Rick Danko.

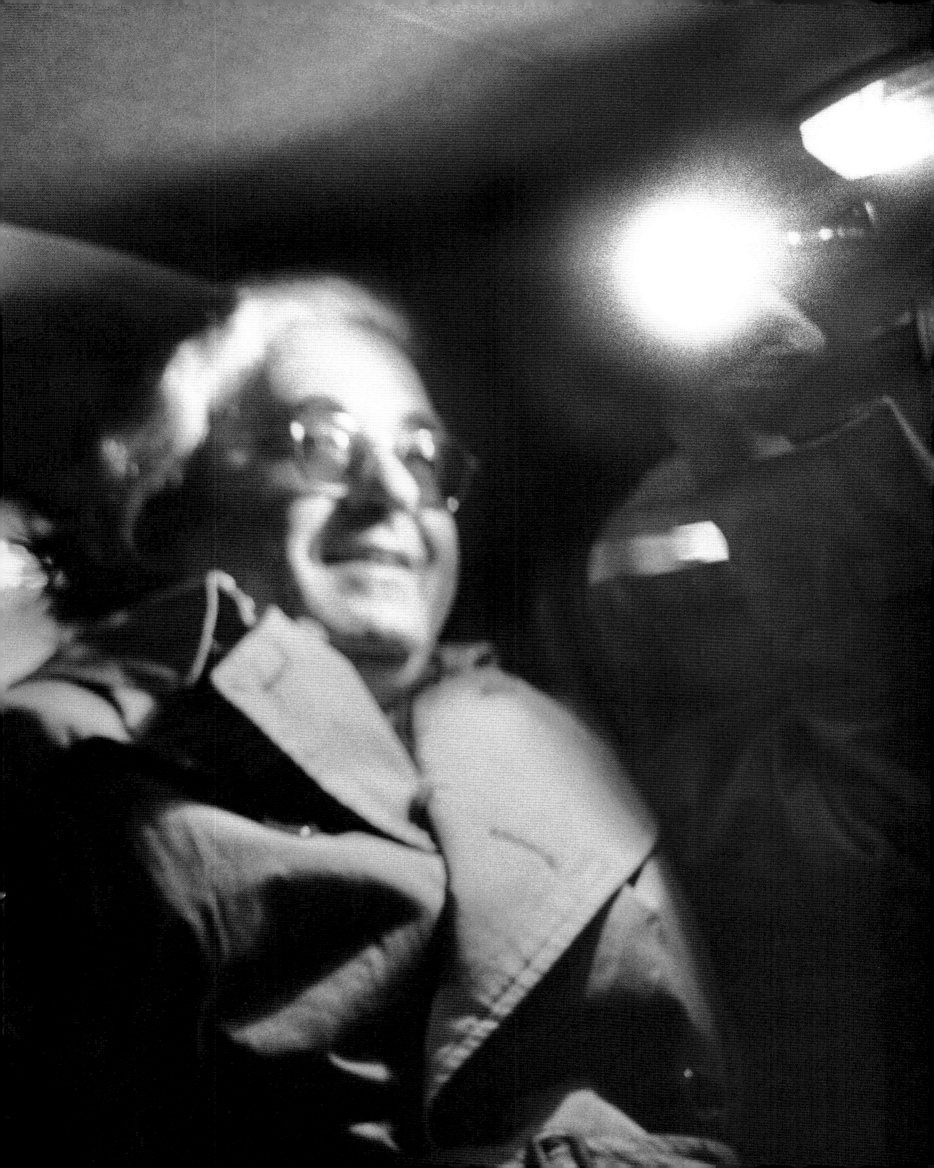

George V Hotel, Paris, 1966

At The George V Hotel in Paris there was a whole bunch of fans screaming for Bob in the street outside. Victor (Maimudes, Dylan's road manager) brought this girl up. She was very elegant and she was so thrilled to meet Bob, like she had died and gone to heaven. She was really nice and she spoke with Bob for a while, a serious conversation with Bob Dylan!

Royal Albert Hall, London, 1966

(previous page)

Bob and Albert leaving the Albert Hall for his hotel, the Mayfair. The show went really well and they were so happy. The Beatles came and there was a party after at the hotel; the Stones were there too. Dylan went to sleep.

Scotland, 1966

England, 1966

"...and don't ever come back!"

George V Hotel, Paris, 1966

(previous page)

In the morning we went to the flea market and Bob bought this puppet. Every time one of the journalists asked him a question, he put his ear to the puppet's mouth and pretended to listen to the answer. Then he would tell the press. It drove them nuts. They didn't understand him.

Backstage, Paris, 1966

(above and right)

This is behind the stage at L'Olympia Theatre in Paris, swapping records and talking with Françoise Hardy. She was very beautiful and a big star in France.

Royal Albert Hall, London, 1966

(right)

Taking a bow at the Albert Hall.

London, 1966

(overleaf)

On the way to the Albert Hall, all these young people were hanging around trying to get a glimpse of him. He was oblivious. They were in such awe of him. He wasn't freaked out though. He understood what it was all about and liked the attention.

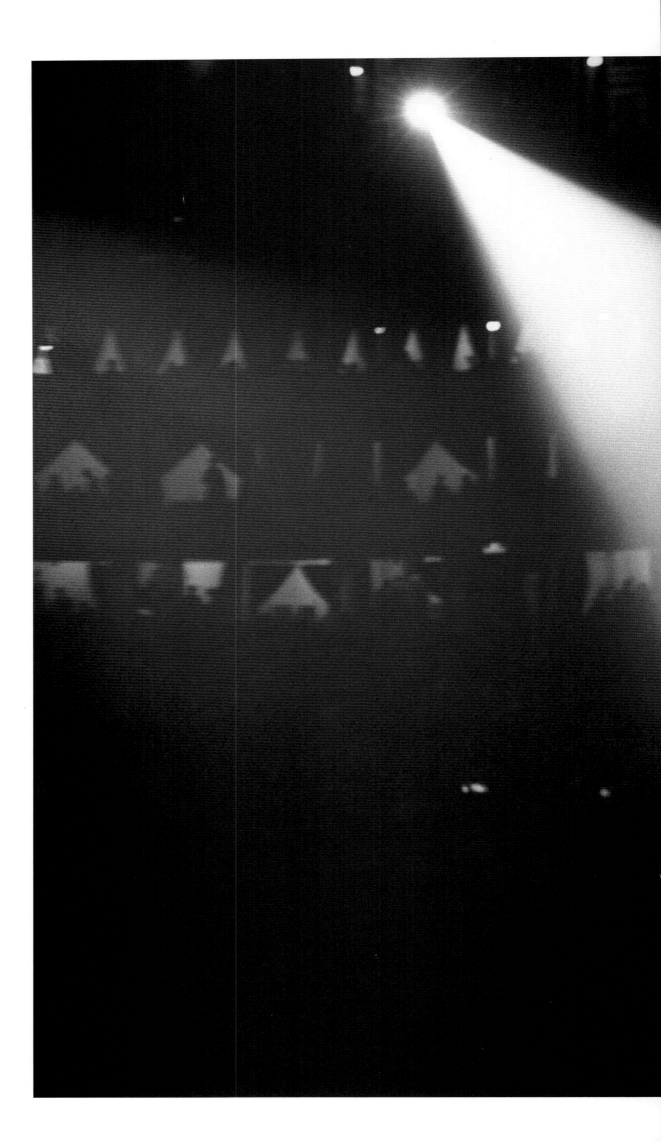

England, 1966

(right and below)

Bob was interested in what
the music press had to say about
him. It didn't really affect him,
but he would get pissed off
once in a while. He was very
quiet about things like that
and didn't give much away
about how he felt.

"The music press
didn't really affect him
but he would get pissed
off once in a while."

Ireland, 1966

Walking through the train, everyone was looking at him. He did look like an alien to them. They were amazed… the suits… he couldn't have cared less.

Birmingham, 1966
(right)

This old lady who sold flowers came in and they really hit it off. He loved to gab with older people.

England, 1966
(left)

On the road there's lots of hanging about. This is Bob with his pal Bob Neuwirth, could be anywhere!

England, 1966
(previous page)

When they were hanging out they would jam; old stuff, new stuff, anything.

Paris, 1966
(left)

After a while all the travelling got boring, but they made it as easy as they could. Pennebaker was always filming them.

"The Aust Ferry shot with the limo is the picture that Bob likes; it told it all. It has depth, he looked cool and it represented the moment."

Bristol, 1966

(this page and overleaf)

11 May, waiting at the Aust Ferry Terminal near Bristol to go to Cardiff in Wales. They chose this shot (overleaf) for the cover of Scorsese's *No Direction Home* CD and DVD. It's one that Bob likes as it told it all. It has depth, he looked cool. I guess he felt it represented the moment to him. Just waiting for the ferry and it turned out to be a good picture.

Leicester, 1966

Bob didn't mind about me being there with my camera. We came to that understanding a long time ago. I was just there, and after a while he got to understand the camera. They were making the *Eat The Document* film at the same time, so he got a good understanding of cameras. I didn't really interact with the film crew; I was on the one side, they were on the other.

Ireland, 1966

(right)

Two Irish ladies got into his room. They were poets and he was quite taken with their poems. It made for a quick friendship.

Edinburgh, 1966

(overleaf)

The hands of a poet. Very expressive. These are the hands that wrote all those great songs.

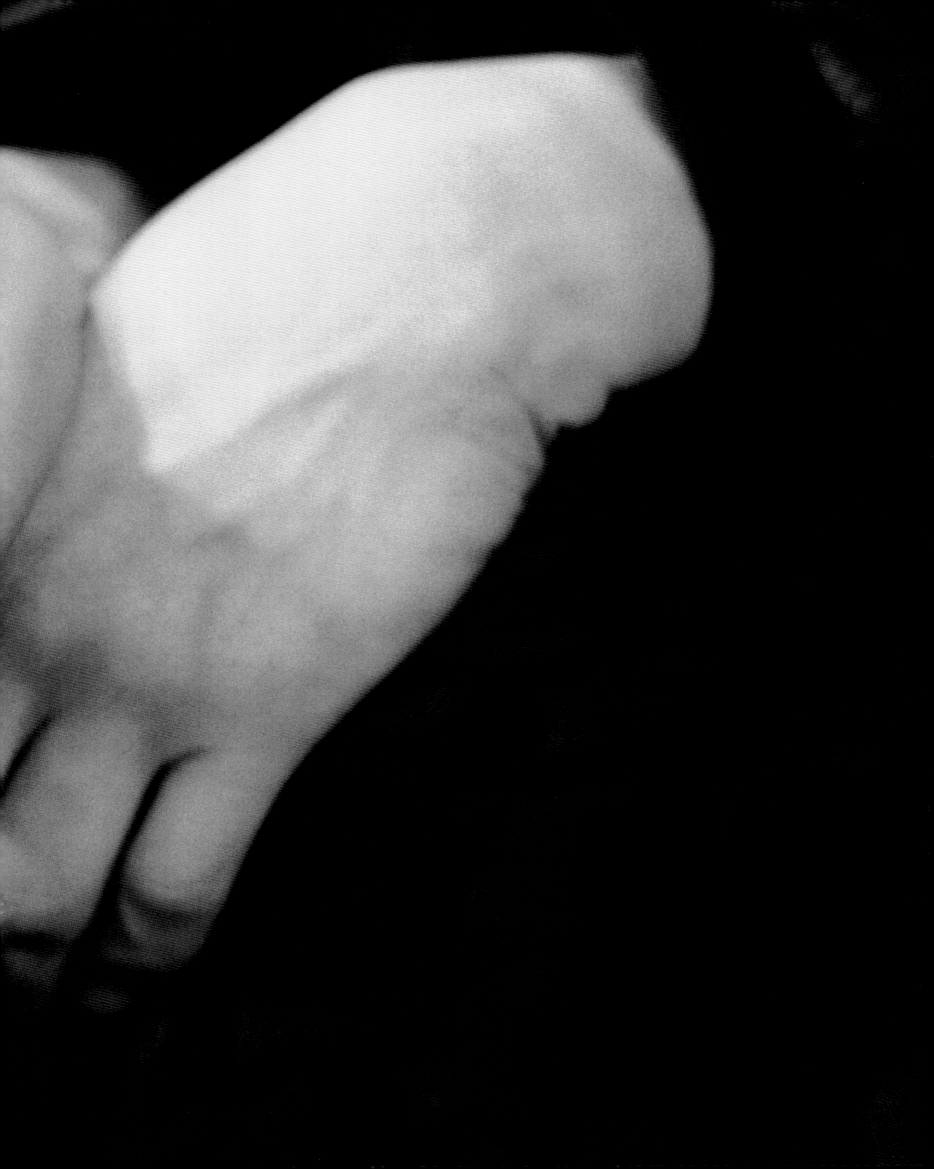

Royal Albert Hall, London, 1966

The band were doing the soundcheck at the Albert Hall, and he was sitting there listening. This made a great photograph; a striking, atmospheric shot. Almost all my Dylan shots were taken unawares. We trusted each other and I captured him as he was at this moment – the loneliness and isolation of being Bob Dylan.

When you make pictures naturally you want to have them published, but you want some mystery to it. Here he is playing guitar on stage at the Albert Hall, there's no mystery, but sitting in the seat, there is a mystery to that. You're giving the public an opportunity to see Bob in a situation they would never ever get to see, even with a ticket.

Scotland, 1966

Everywhere we went, in situations like this when he got out in the street, people would follow him. It wasn't a drag, but he wasn't in the anonymous business!

Scotland, 1966

Savoy Hotel, London, 1966

Bob would pick up the movie camera, turn the tables and film things. The band are checking him out.

Birmingham, 1966
(previous page)

Knock, knock, knocking on
heaven's door...

England, 1966
(left)

Leicester, 1966
(right)

Paris, 1966
(below)

Dublin, 1966

Bob on the telephone in his hotel suite. He was looking at some sheet music and holding a razor, but I don't think there is any significance in it!

England, 1966

Paris, 1966

(previous page)

The press followed him
everywhere in Paris. This
guy was on the the back of a
motorcycle, camera and flash
at the ready, no crash helmet!

Ireland, 1966

(right)

Paris, 1966

24 May, Bob's birthday in Paris.
After the show, we had a surprise
party with a cake and everything.

Paris, 1966

(previous page)

L'Olympia in Paris is like
the national music hall or
something, and they thought it
was pretty out there to hang the
Stars and Stripes. Bob only used
it there and nowhere else.

Royal Albert
Hall, London, 1966

Rehearsing at the Albert Hall.

England, 1966

Bob getting ready for take off on the tarmac with drummer Mickey Jones, bassist Rick Danko and guitarist Robbie Robertson.

Dylan & The Band Tour, 1974

(right and overleaf)

Years later, same procedure, different airport. This was the Starship [overleaf], used by Led Zeppelin and everyone, very luxurious, bedrooms, bars and VCRs. Anything you needed was on that plane and there were only 11 of us on it. This tour was different from '66, very controlled. Everything was taken care of and very easy. You were picked up, driven to an airport, and picked up the other end, given hotel room keys and the fictitious name you were using. We all knew each other by our made-up names.

Although much had changed in the industry, like bigger venues and sound systems, it was pretty much the same for me as before. I had the same access and worked in the same way and even used the same cameras.

Chicago, 1974

(left)

The tour started in Chicago in the winter. It was cold. Bob looks more like a sheikh than a singer.

Washington, 1974

(below)

We visited the Philips Collection, a small museum in Dupont Circle.

Washington, 1974

Bob and an El Greco painting.

"Jimmy Carter was a big fan of Bob's and they really hit it off."

Washington, 1974
(above)

Jimmy Carter invited us for breakfast at the governor's mansion. He was a delightful man. We stayed there 'til four in the morning or something. He was a big fan of Bob's and they really hit it off.

On Tour, 1974
(right)

Playing chess on The Starship.

Los Angeles, 1974
(right)

Los Angeles, 1974
(overleaf)

Bob's lying down, relaxing
before the show, taking it easy.

Los Angeles, 1974

The LA Forum. I stood there and said, 'I'm not moving 'til you smile!' Bob smiled.

LA Forum, 1974

The audience went
crazy on this tour.

Dylan & The Band Tour, 1974

After this tour ended I said I would never go on another tour again because it would never be as great as this.

Exclusive Distributors
Music Sales Limited
14 -15 Berners Street
London, W1T 3LJ
England

Music Sales Corporation
257 Park Avenue South
New York, NY 10010, USA

Macmillan Distribution Services
53 Park West Drive
Derrimut, Vic 3030
Australia

Printed in Thailand

A catalogue record for this book is available from the British Library.

Visit Omnibus Press on the web at www.omnibuspress.com

Music Sales Limited is a Registered Company in England under
Company No. 315155. VAT Registration No. 417691828

A full list of Directors is available at the company's registered office:
14-15 Berners Street, London W1T 3LJ, England.